St. Margaret Mary Library
7813 Shelbyville Rd.
Louisville, KY 40222

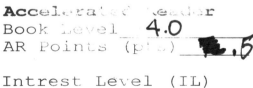

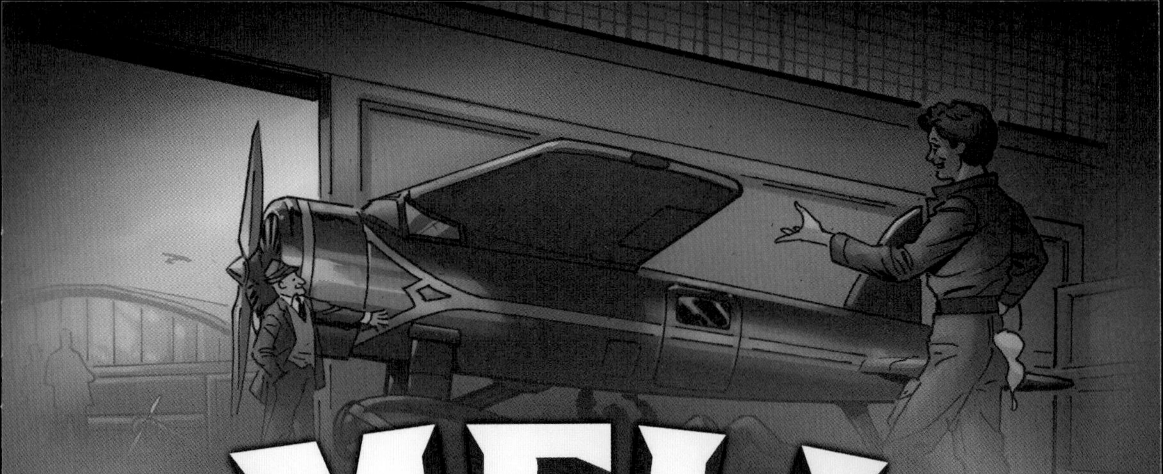

AMELIA EARHART

FLIES ACROSS THE ATLANTIC

By Nel Yomtov

Illustration By Tod Smith

Color By Gerardo Sandoval

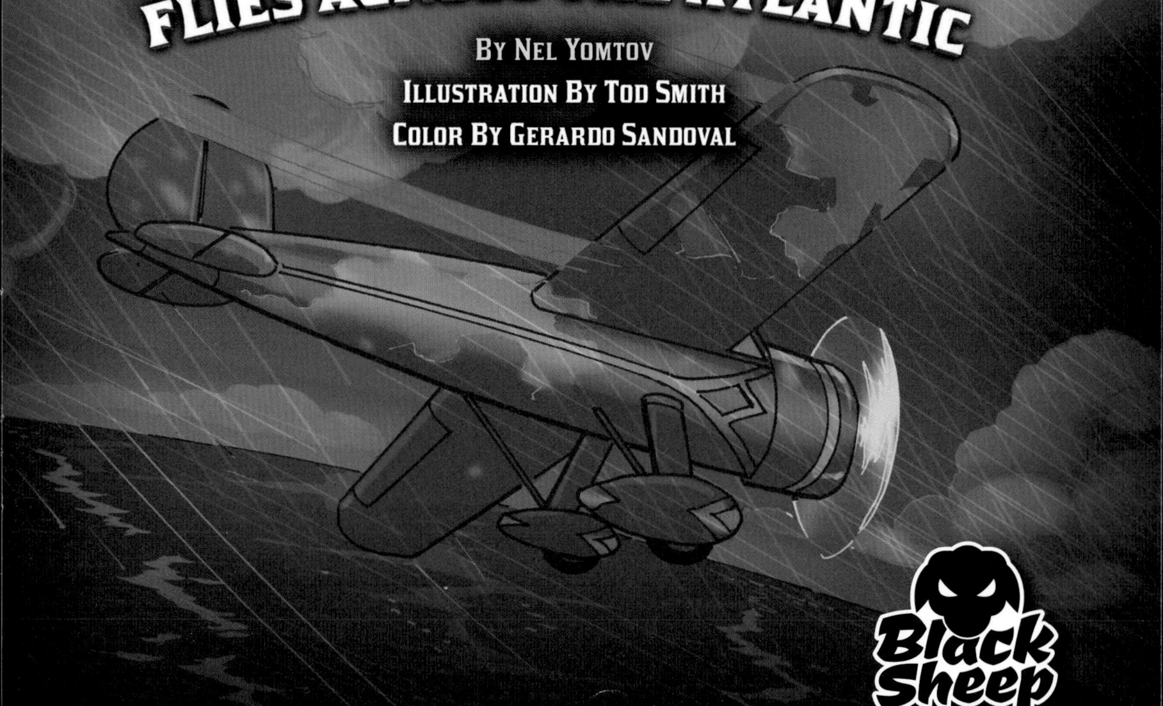

Black Sheep

BELLWETHER MEDIA • MINNEAPOLIS, MN

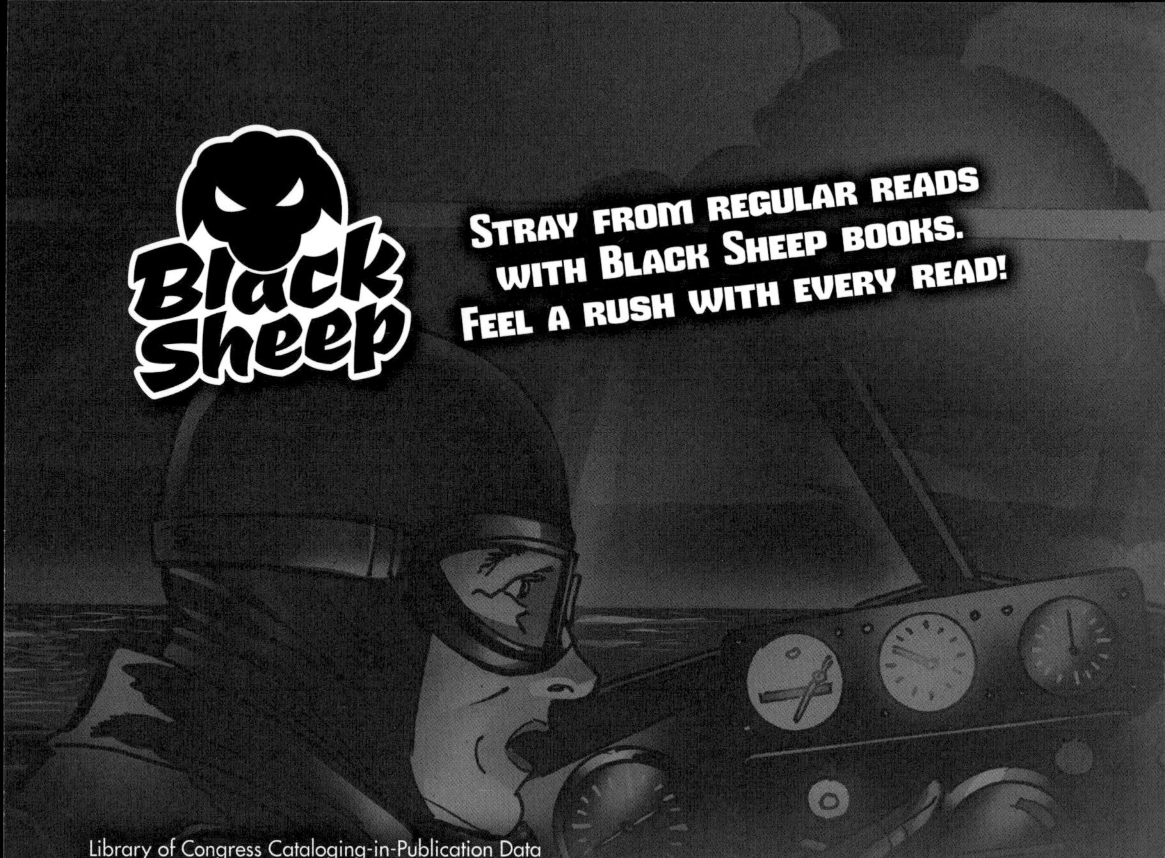
Black Sheep
STRAY FROM REGULAR READS
WITH BLACK SHEEP BOOKS.
FEEL A RUSH WITH EVERY READ!

Library of Congress Cataloging-in-Publication Data

Yomtov, Nelson.
Amelia Earhart Flies Across the Atlantic / by Nel Yomtov.
pages cm. -- (Black sheep: Extraordinary Explorers)
Summary: "Exciting illustrations follow the events of Amelia Earhart's flight across the Atlantic. The combination of brightly colored panels and leveled text is intended for students in grades 3 through 7"-- Provided by publisher.
Audience: Ages 7 to 12
In graphic novel form.
Includes bibliographical references and index.
ISBN 978-1-62617-290-6 (hardcover: alk. paper)
1. Earhart, Amelia, 1897-1937--Juvenile literature. 2. Air pilots--United States--Biography--Juvenile literature. 3. Women air pilots--United States--Biography--Juvenile literature. 4. Transatlantic flights--Juvenile literature. I. Title.
TL540.E3Y66 2016
629.13092--dc23
[B]

2015015375

This edition first published in 2016 by Bellwether Media, Inc.

Printed in the United States of America, North Mankato, MN.

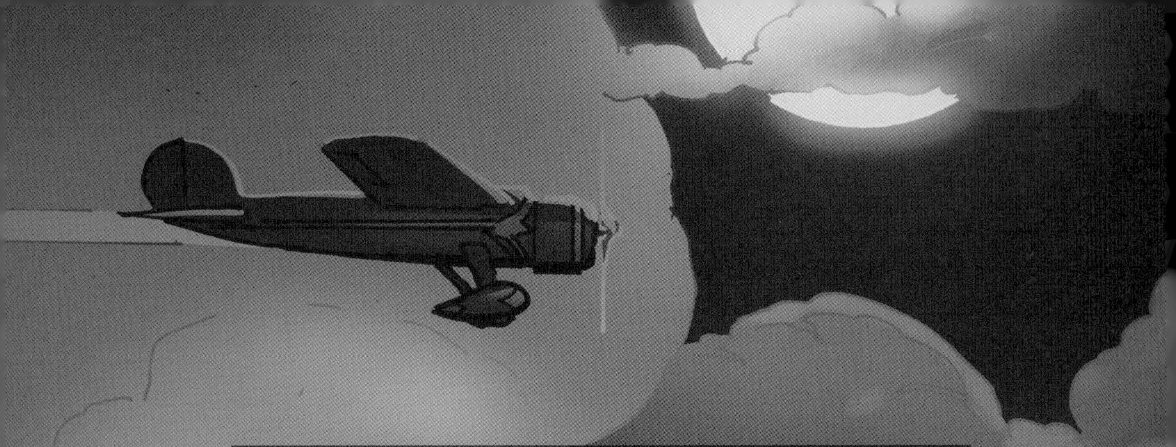

TABLE OF CONTENTS

WINGS ACROSS THE ATLANTIC   4

INTO THE STORM   8

THE DANGERS MOUNT   12

A SAFE LANDING   18

MORE ABOUT AMELIA EARHART   22

GLOSSARY   23

TO LEARN MORE   24

INDEX   24

Red text identifies historical quotes.

Wings Across the Atlantic

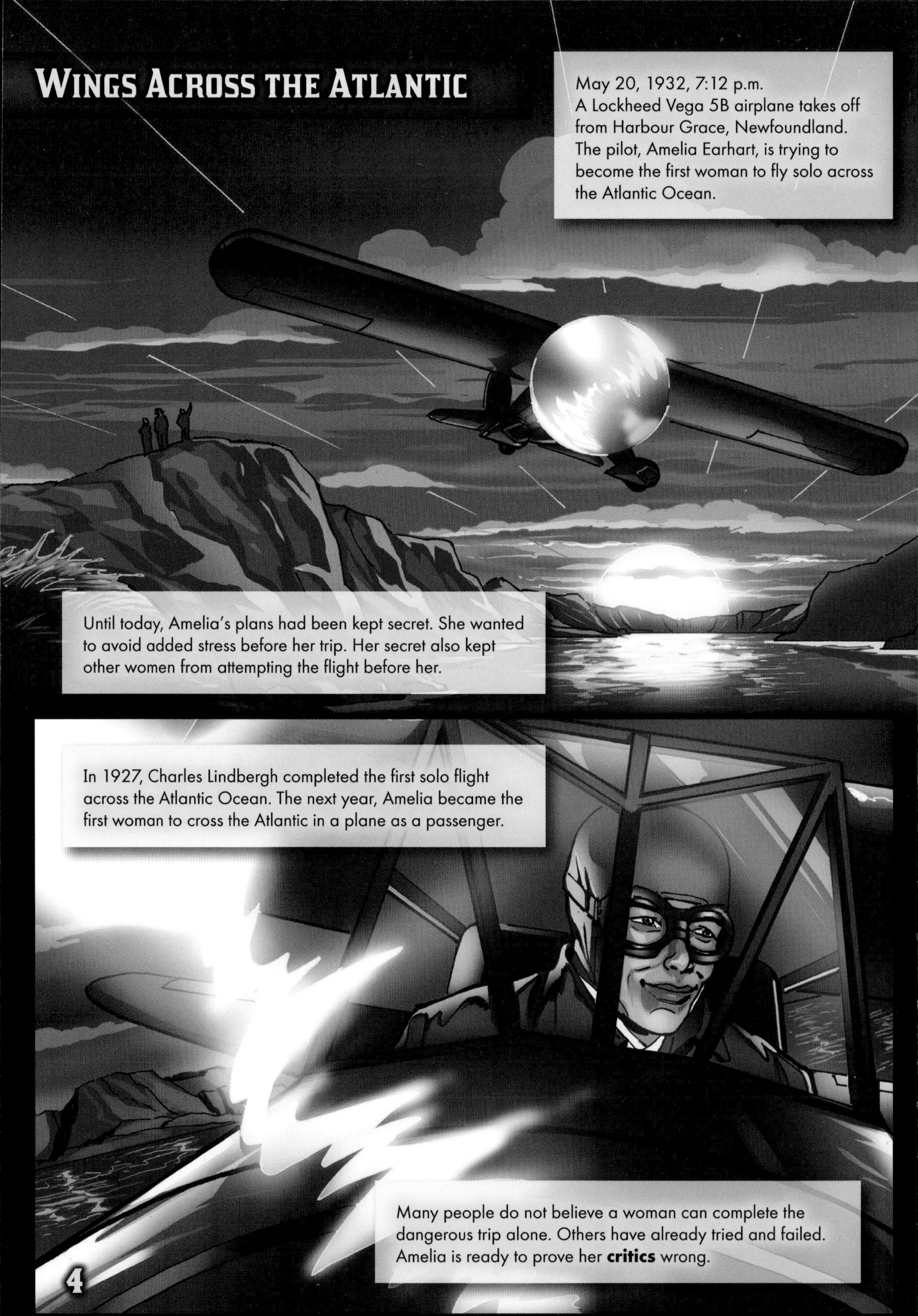
May 20, 1932, 7:12 p.m.
A Lockheed Vega 5B airplane takes off from Harbour Grace, Newfoundland. The pilot, Amelia Earhart, is trying to become the first woman to fly solo across the Atlantic Ocean.
Until today, Amelia's plans had been kept secret. She wanted to avoid added stress before her trip. Her secret also kept other women from attempting the flight before her.
In 1927, Charles Lindbergh completed the first solo flight across the Atlantic Ocean. The next year, Amelia became the first woman to cross the Atlantic in a plane as a passenger.
Many people do not believe a woman can complete the dangerous trip alone. Others have already tried and failed. Amelia is ready to prove her **critics** wrong.

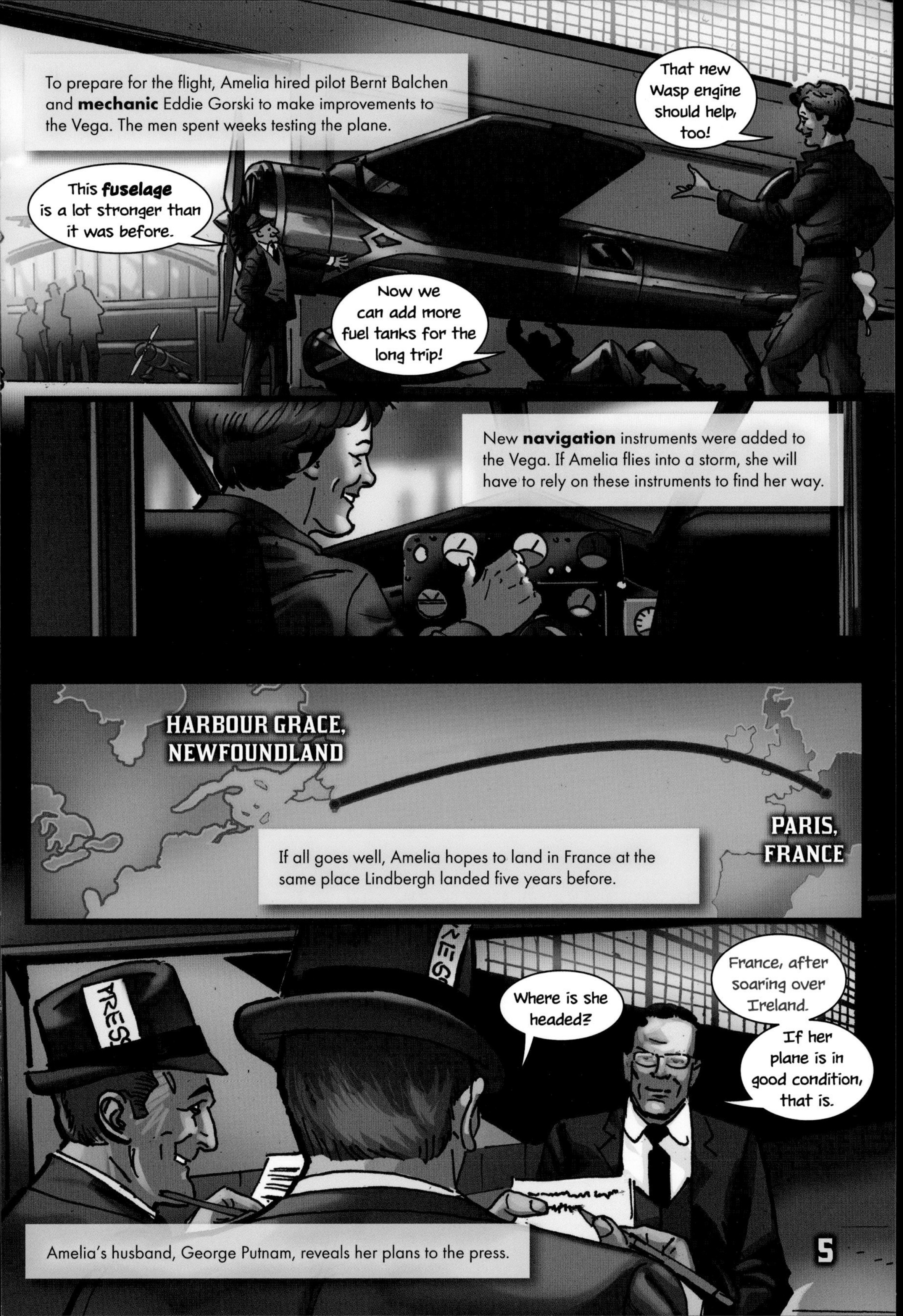
To prepare for the flight, Amelia hired pilot Bernt Balchen and **mechanic** Eddie Gorski to make improvements to the Vega. The men spent weeks testing the plane.
That new Wasp engine should help, too!
This **fuselage** is a lot stronger than it was before.
Now we can add more fuel tanks for the long trip!
New **navigation** instruments were added to the Vega. If Amelia flies into a storm, she will have to rely on these instruments to find her way.
HARBOUR GRACE, NEWFOUNDLAND
PARIS, FRANCE
If all goes well, Amelia hopes to land in France at the same place Lindbergh landed five years before.
PRESS
Where is she headed?
France, after soaring over Ireland.
If her plane is in good condition, that is.
Amelia's husband, George Putnam, reveals her plans to the press.

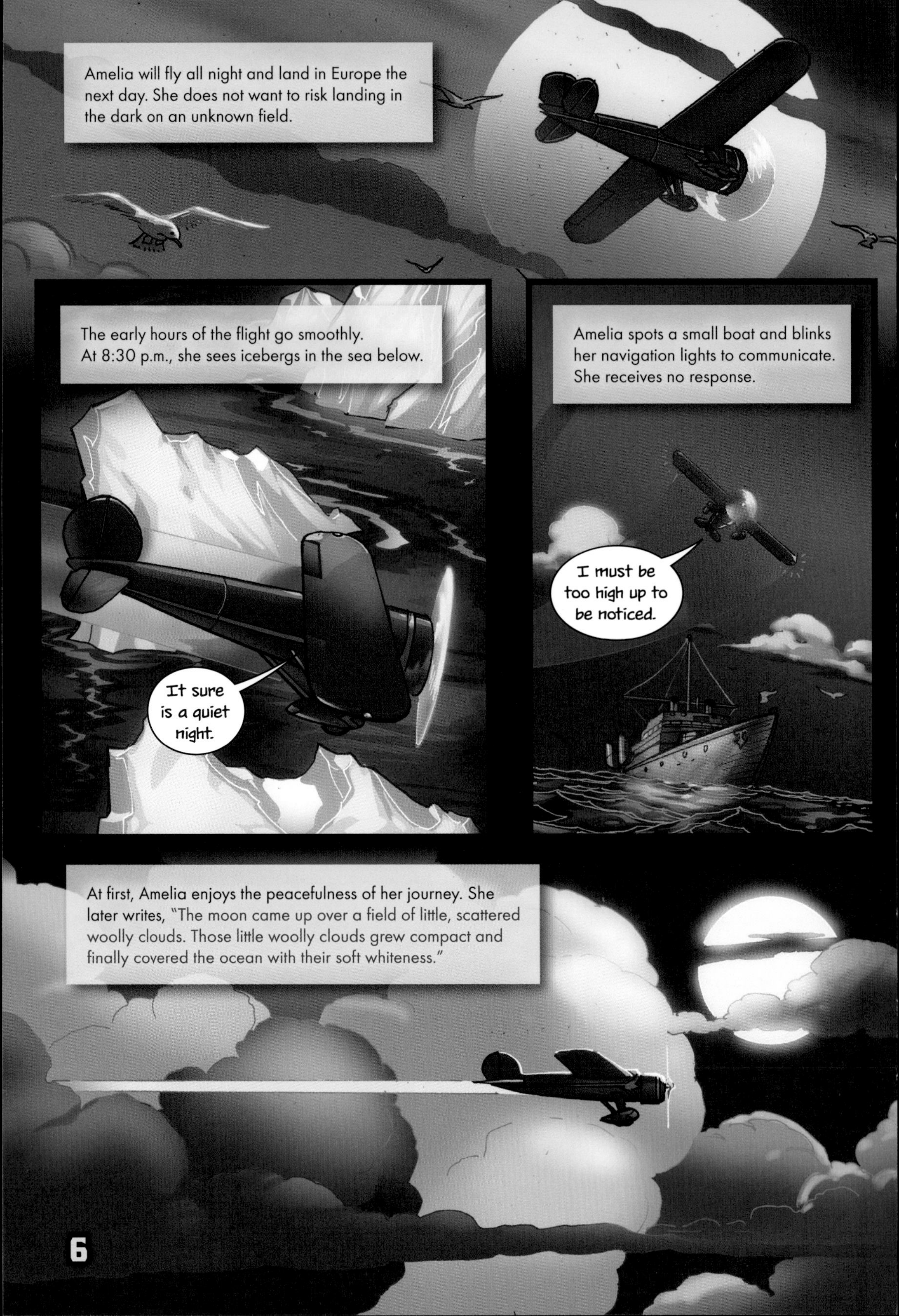

Amelia will fly all night and land in Europe the next day. She does not want to risk landing in the dark on an unknown field.

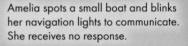

The early hours of the flight go smoothly. At 8:30 p.m., she sees icebergs in the sea below.

It sure is a quiet night.

Amelia spots a small boat and blinks her navigation lights to communicate. She receives no response.

I must be too high up to be noticed.

At first, Amelia enjoys the peacefulness of her journey. She later writes, "The moon came up over a field of little, scattered woolly clouds. Those little woolly clouds grew compact and finally covered the ocean with their soft whiteness."

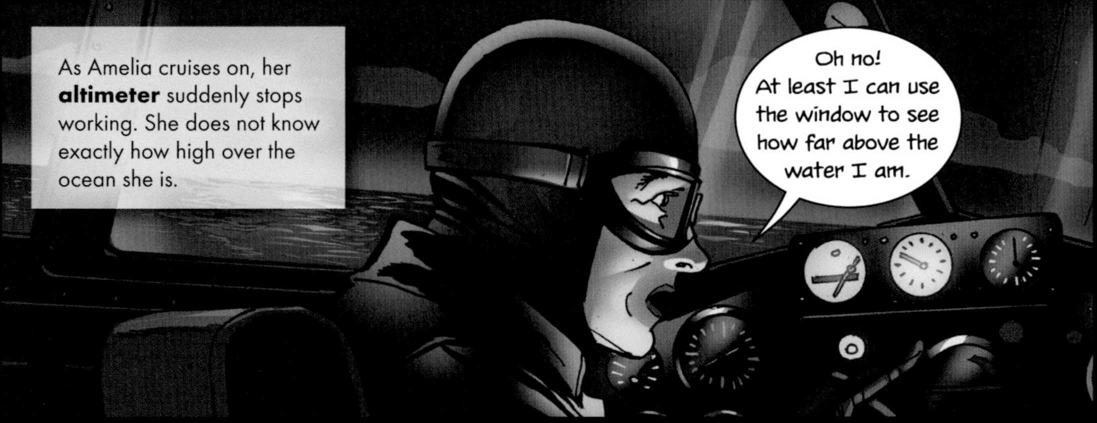
As Amelia cruises on, her **altimeter** suddenly stops working. She does not know exactly how high over the ocean she is.
Oh no! At least I can use the window to see how far above the water I am.

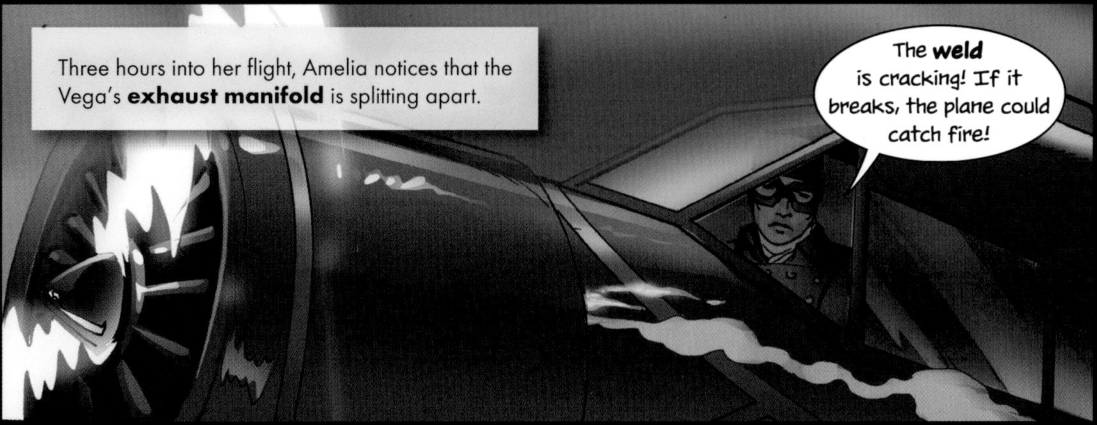
Three hours into her flight, Amelia notices that the Vega's **exhaust manifold** is splitting apart.
The **weld** is cracking! If it breaks, the plane could catch fire!

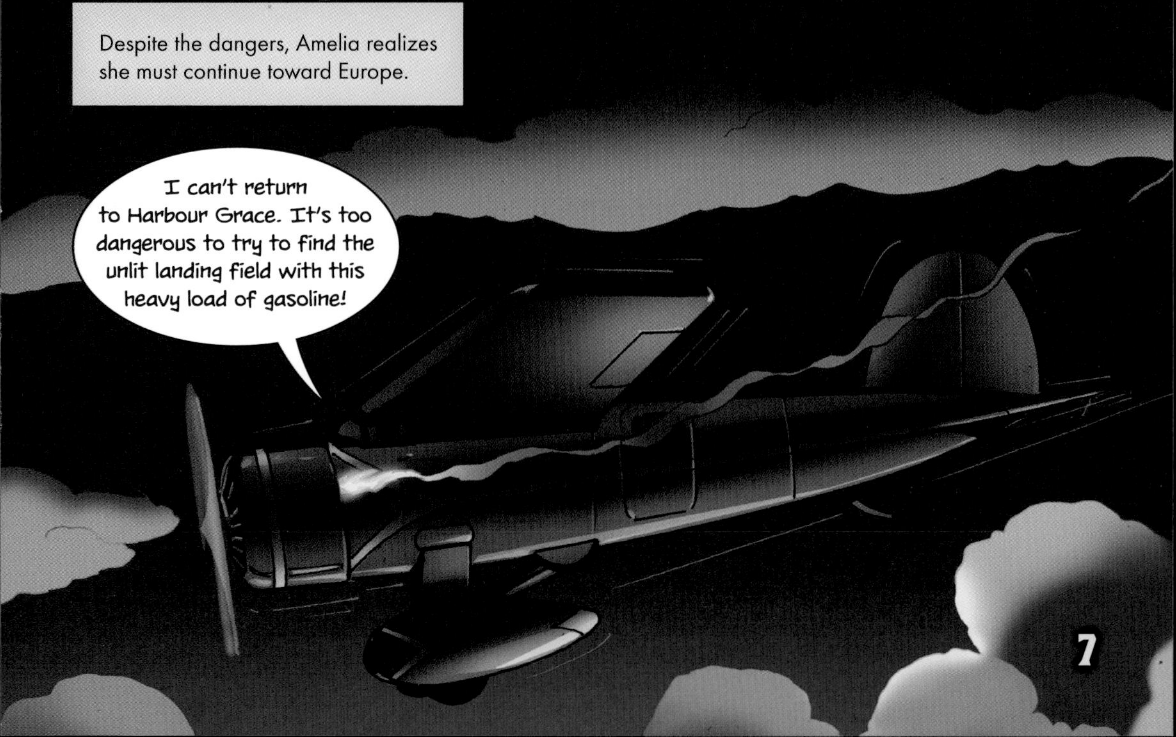
Despite the dangers, Amelia realizes she must continue toward Europe.
I can't return to Harbour Grace. It's too dangerous to try to find the unlit landing field with this heavy load of gasoline!

Into the Storm

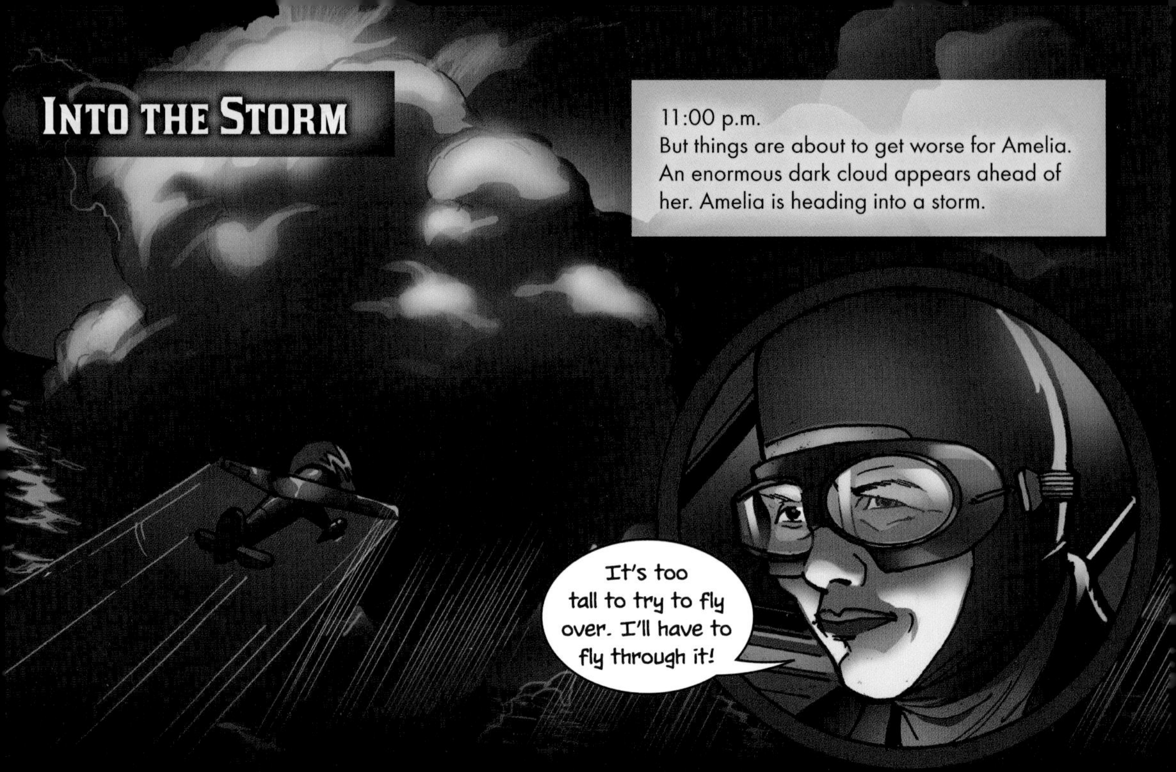
11:00 p.m.
But things are about to get worse for Amelia. An enormous dark cloud appears ahead of her. Amelia is heading into a storm.
It's too tall to try to fly over. I'll have to fly through it!

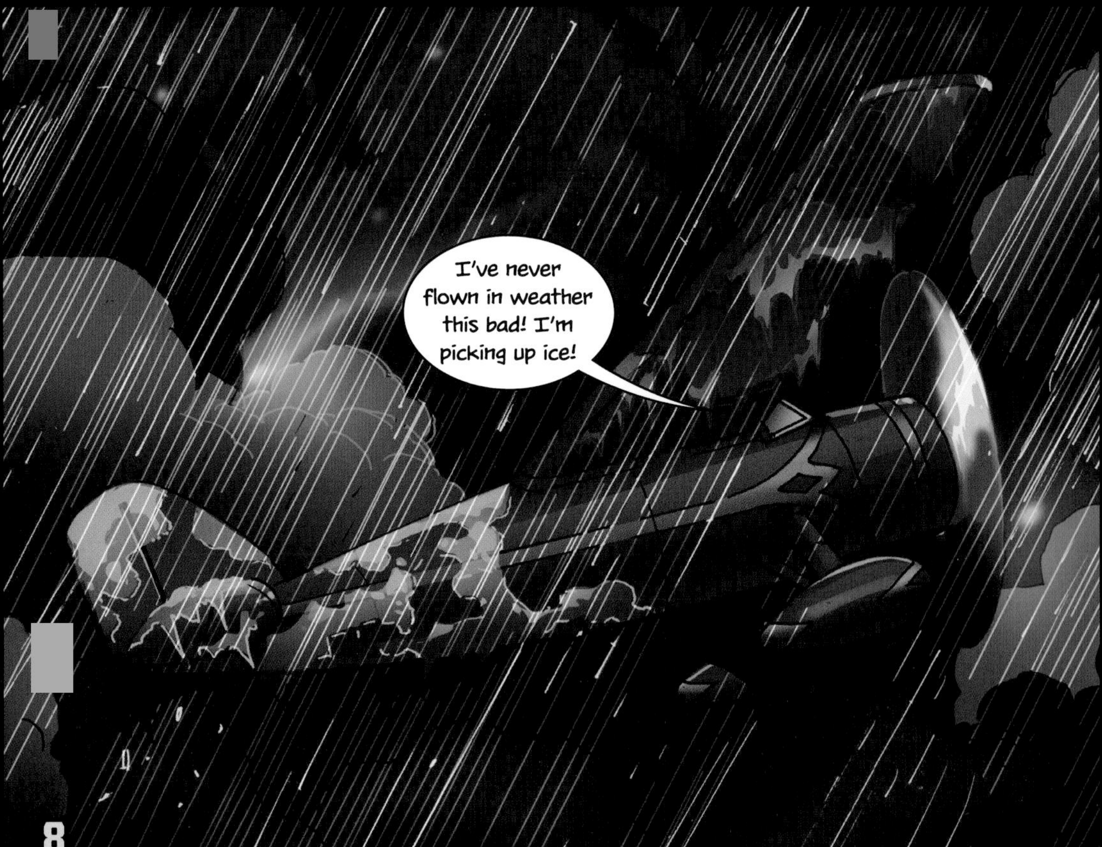
I've never flown in weather this bad! I'm picking up ice!

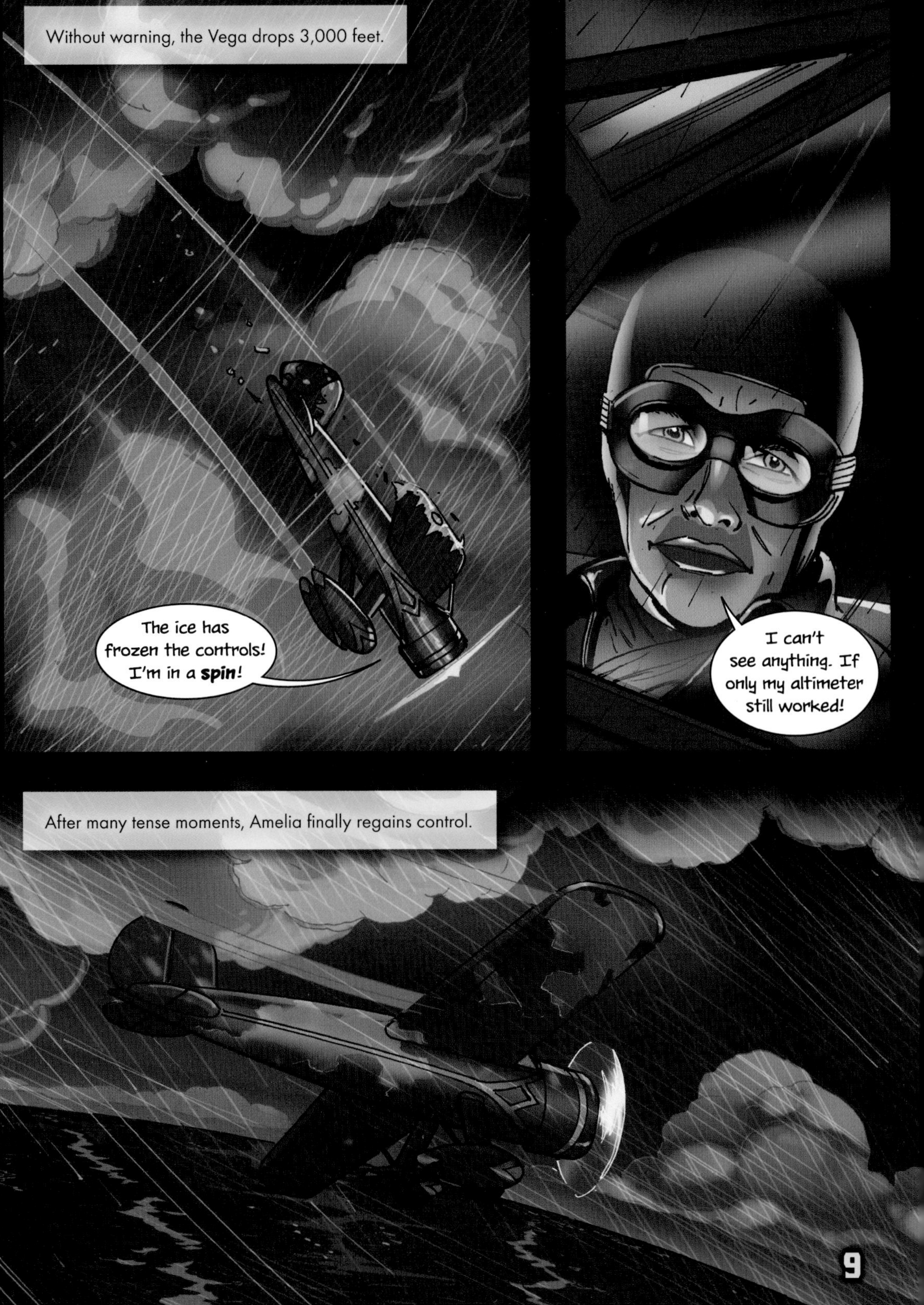
Without warning, the Vega drops 3,000 feet.
The ice has frozen the controls! I'm in a **spin**!
I can't see anything. If only my altimeter still worked!
After many tense moments, Amelia finally regains control.

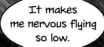

It makes me nervous flying so low.

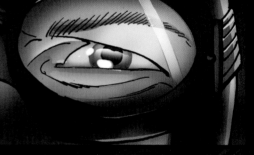

As Amelia flies near the surface of the water, she hits a low patch of fog.

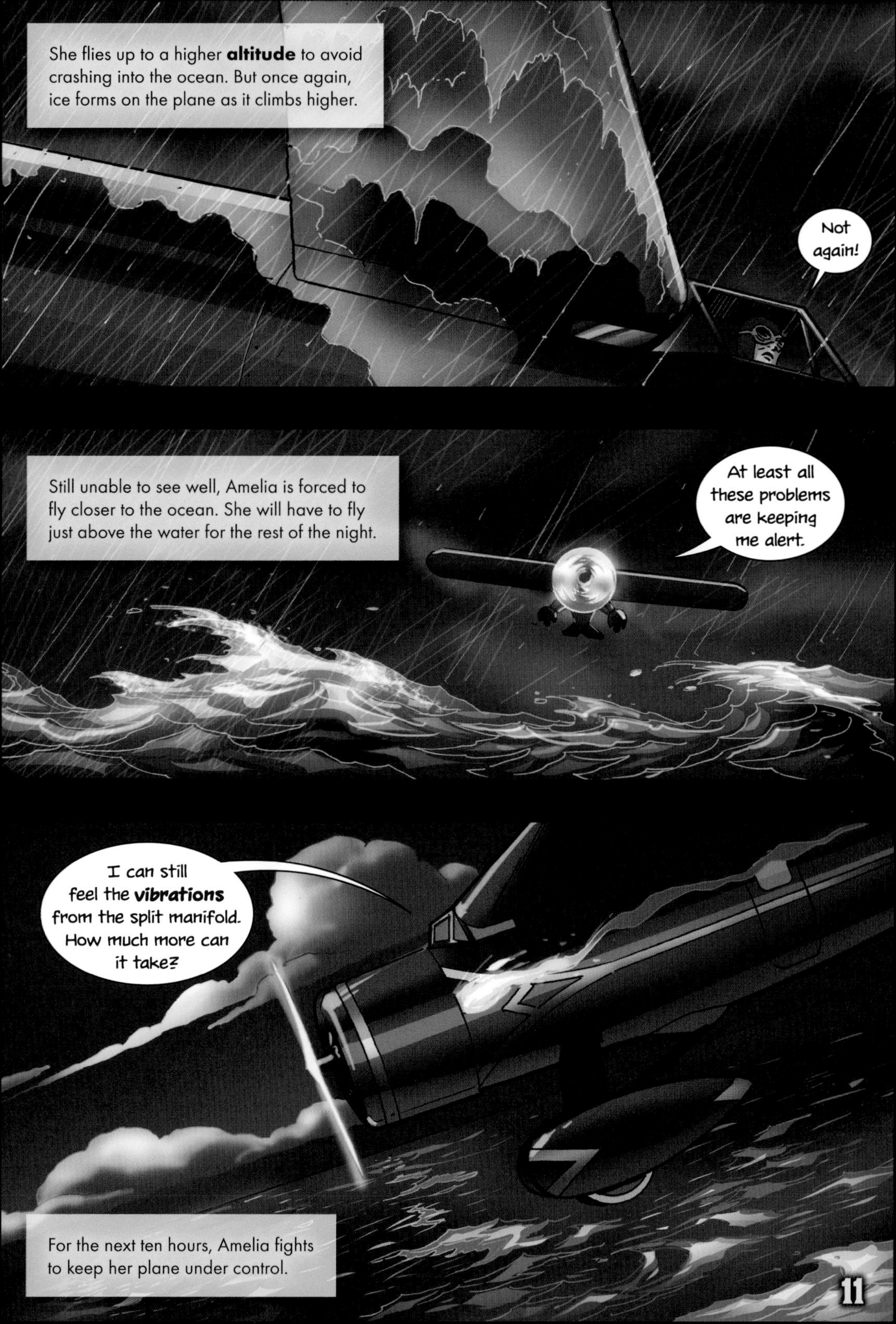
She flies up to a higher **altitude** to avoid crashing into the ocean. But once again, ice forms on the plane as it climbs higher.
Not again!
Still unable to see well, Amelia is forced to fly closer to the ocean. She will have to fly just above the water for the rest of the night.
At least all these problems are keeping me alert.
I can still feel the **vibrations** from the split manifold. How much more can it take?
For the next ten hours, Amelia fights to keep her plane under control.

The Dangers Mount

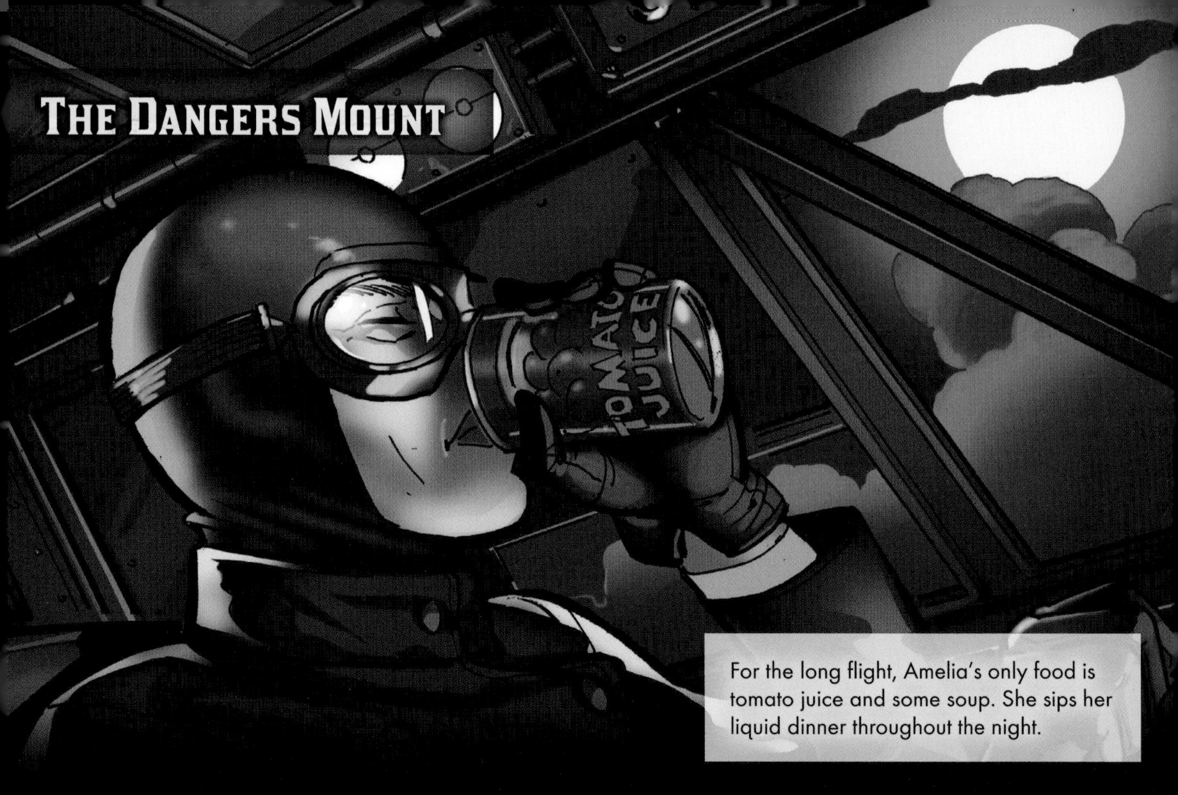
TOMATO JUICE
For the long flight, Amelia's only food is tomato juice and some soup. She sips her liquid dinner throughout the night.

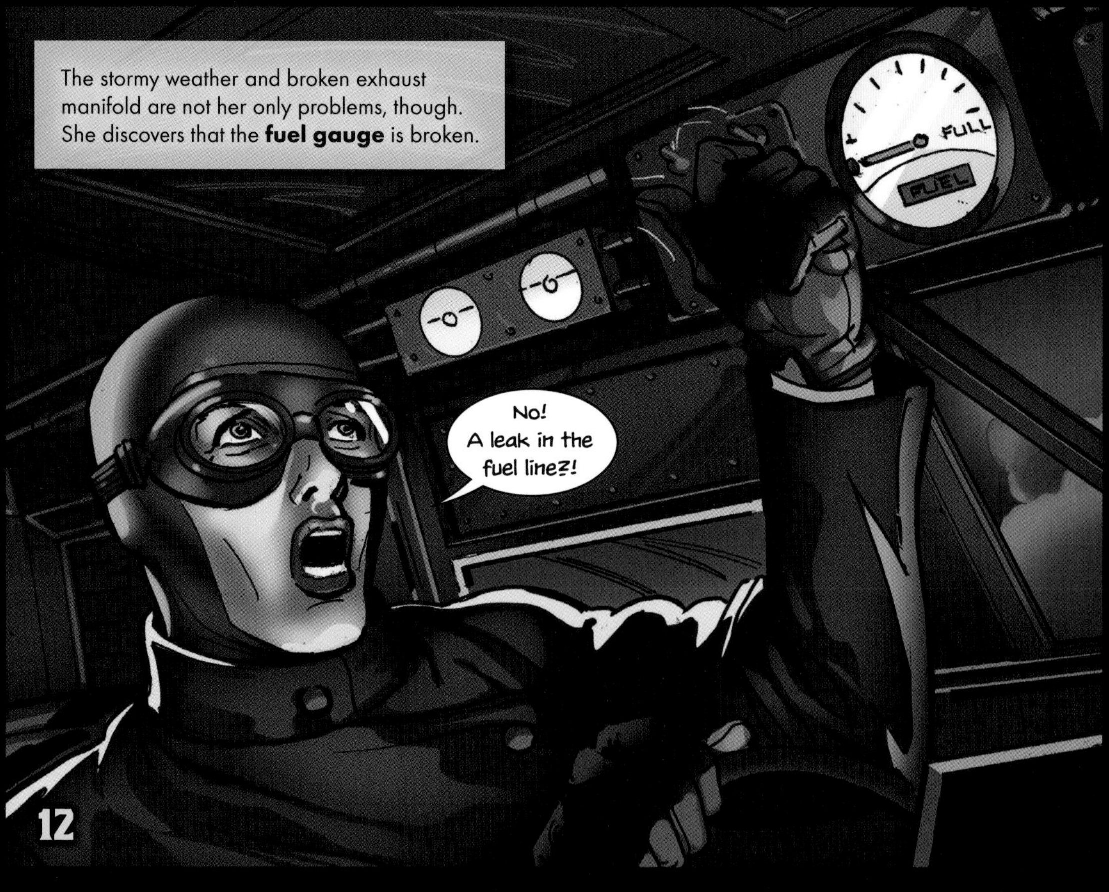
The stormy weather and broken exhaust manifold are not her only problems, though. She discovers that the **fuel gauge** is broken.
FULL
FUEL
No! A leak in the fuel line?!

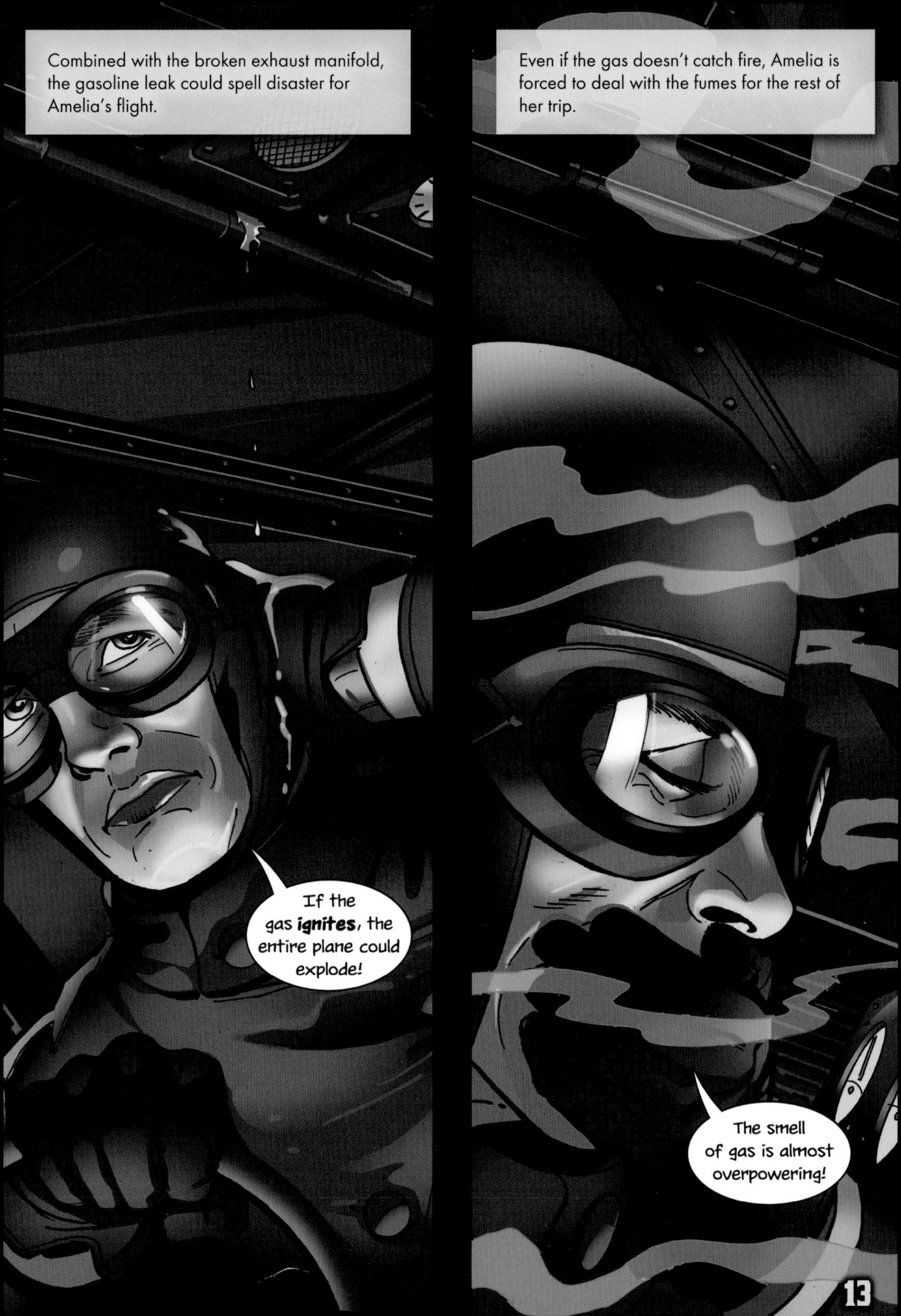
Combined with the broken exhaust manifold, the gasoline leak could spell disaster for Amelia's flight.
If the gas **ignites**, the entire plane could explode!
Even if the gas doesn't catch fire, Amelia is forced to deal with the fumes for the rest of her trip.
The smell of gas is almost overpowering!

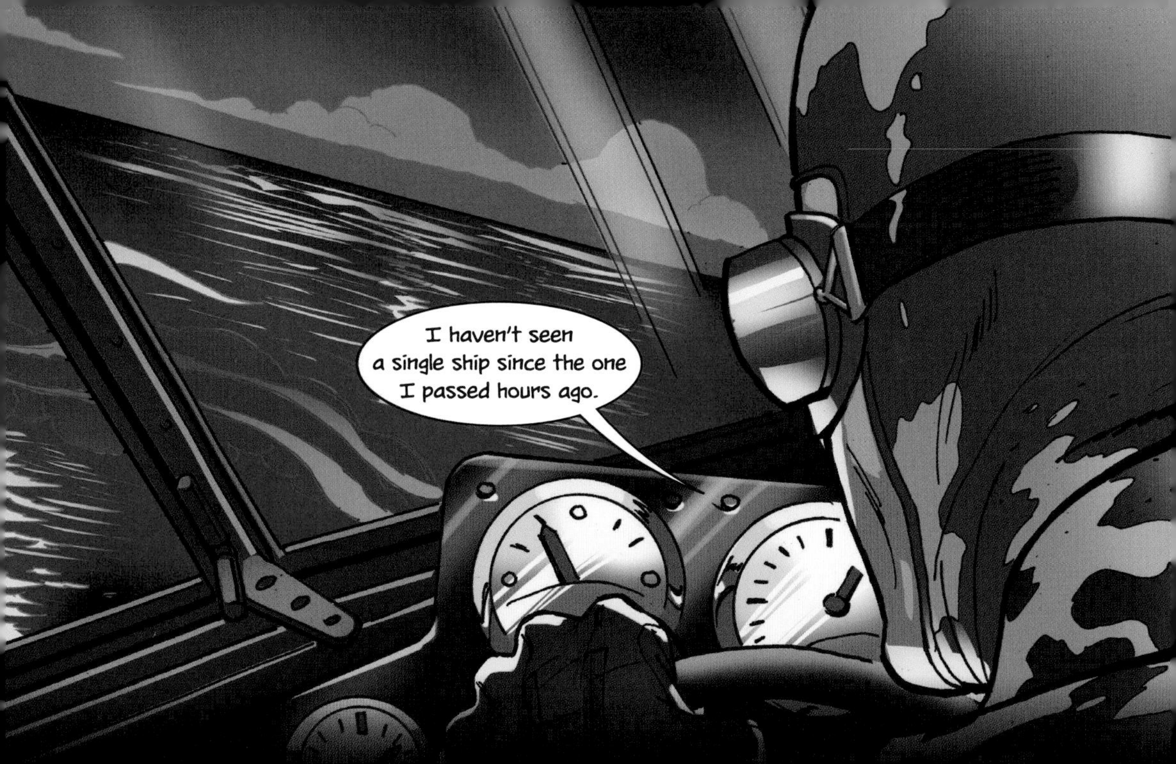
I haven't seen a single ship since the one I passed hours ago.

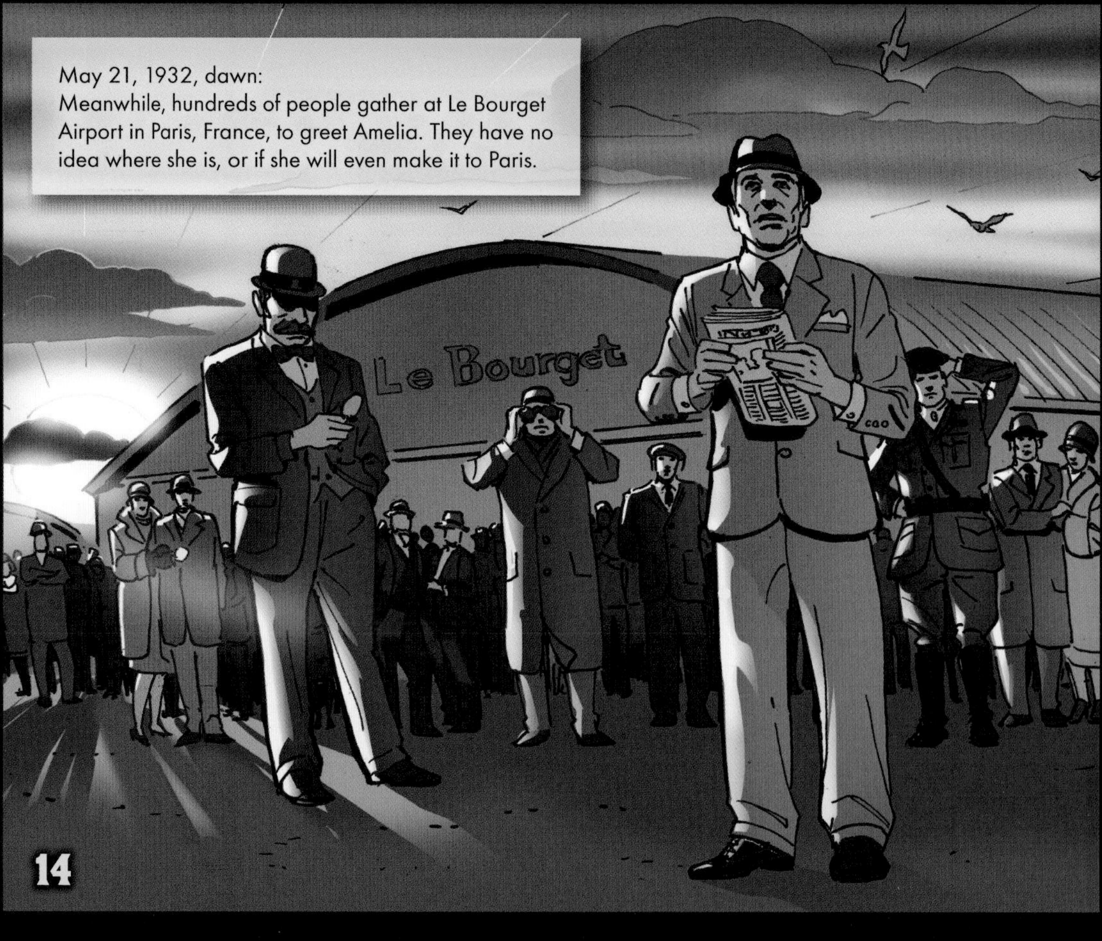
May 21, 1932, dawn:
Meanwhile, hundreds of people gather at Le Bourget Airport in Paris, France, to greet Amelia. They have no idea where she is, or if she will even make it to Paris.
Le Bourget

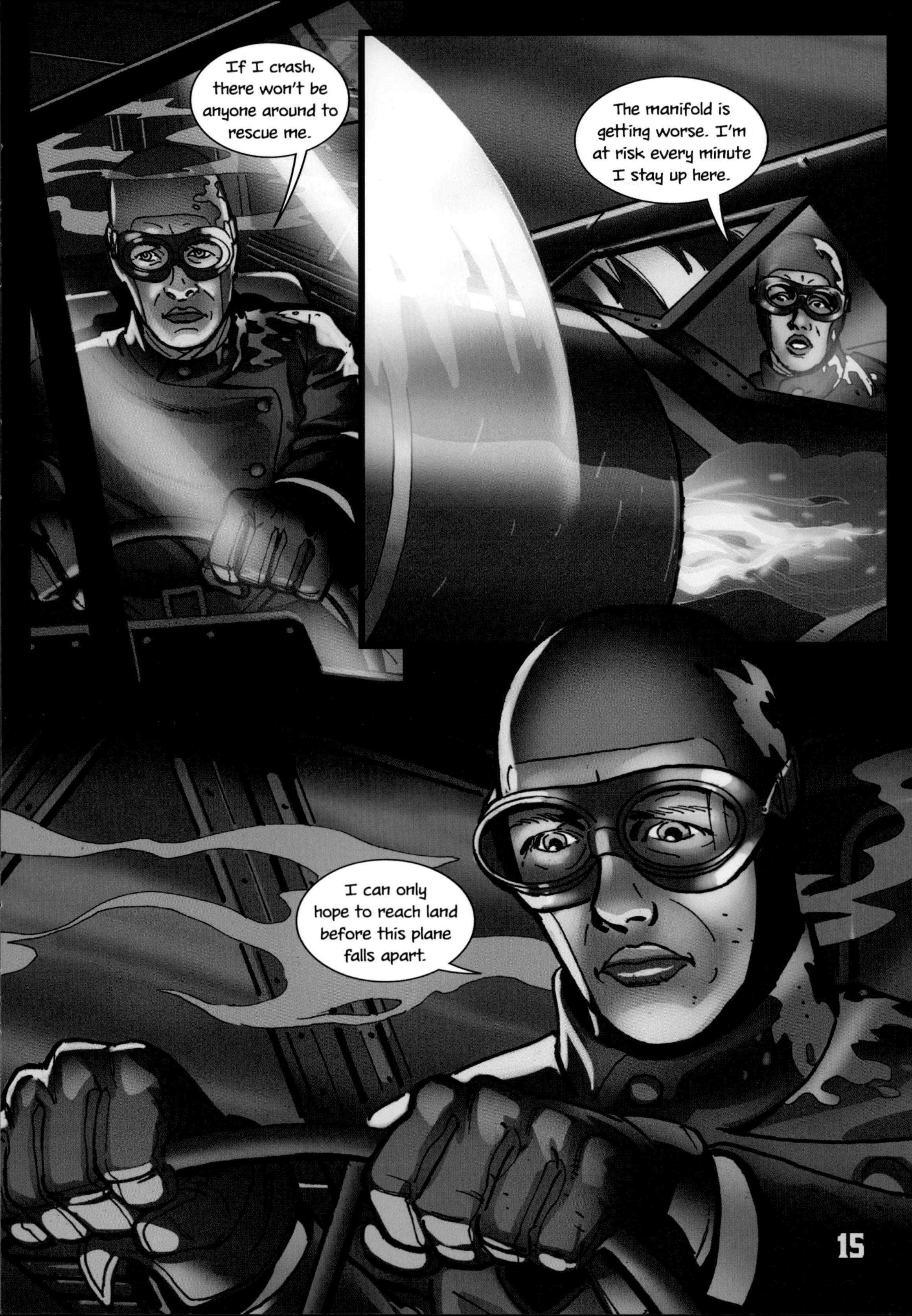
If I crash, there won't be anyone around to rescue me.
The manifold is getting worse. I'm at risk every minute I stay up here.
I can only hope to reach land before this plane falls apart.

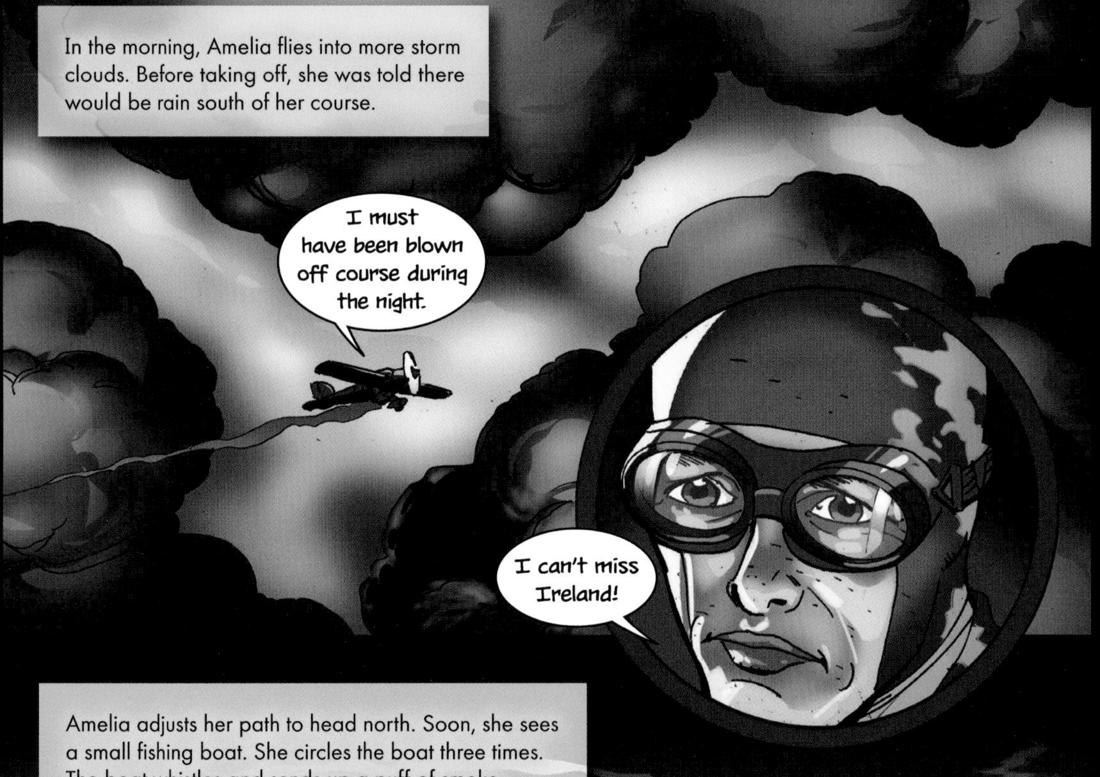
In the morning, Amelia flies into more storm clouds. Before taking off, she was told there would be rain south of her course.
I must have been blown off course during the night.
I can't miss Ireland!

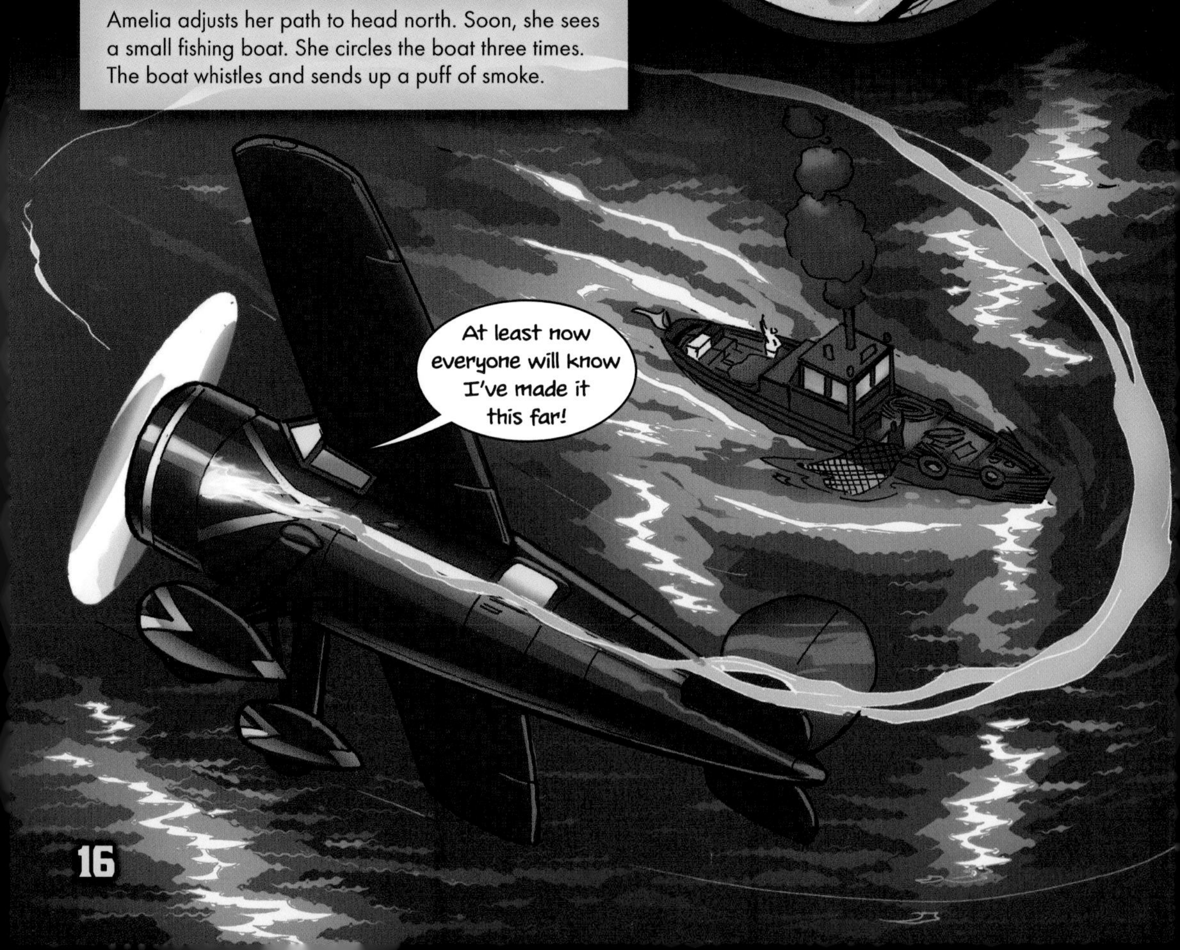
Amelia adjusts her path to head north. Soon, she sees a small fishing boat. She circles the boat three times. The boat whistles and sends up a puff of smoke.
At least now everyone will know I've made it this far!

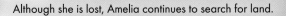

Although she is lost, Amelia continues to search for land.

I can't risk flying this plane much farther. I need to find an airport!

Land! At last!

Amelia runs into thunderstorms above the coastal mountains. She wisely chooses not to risk flying through them.

I'll have to keep going north. I really hope my fuel will last!

A Safe Landing

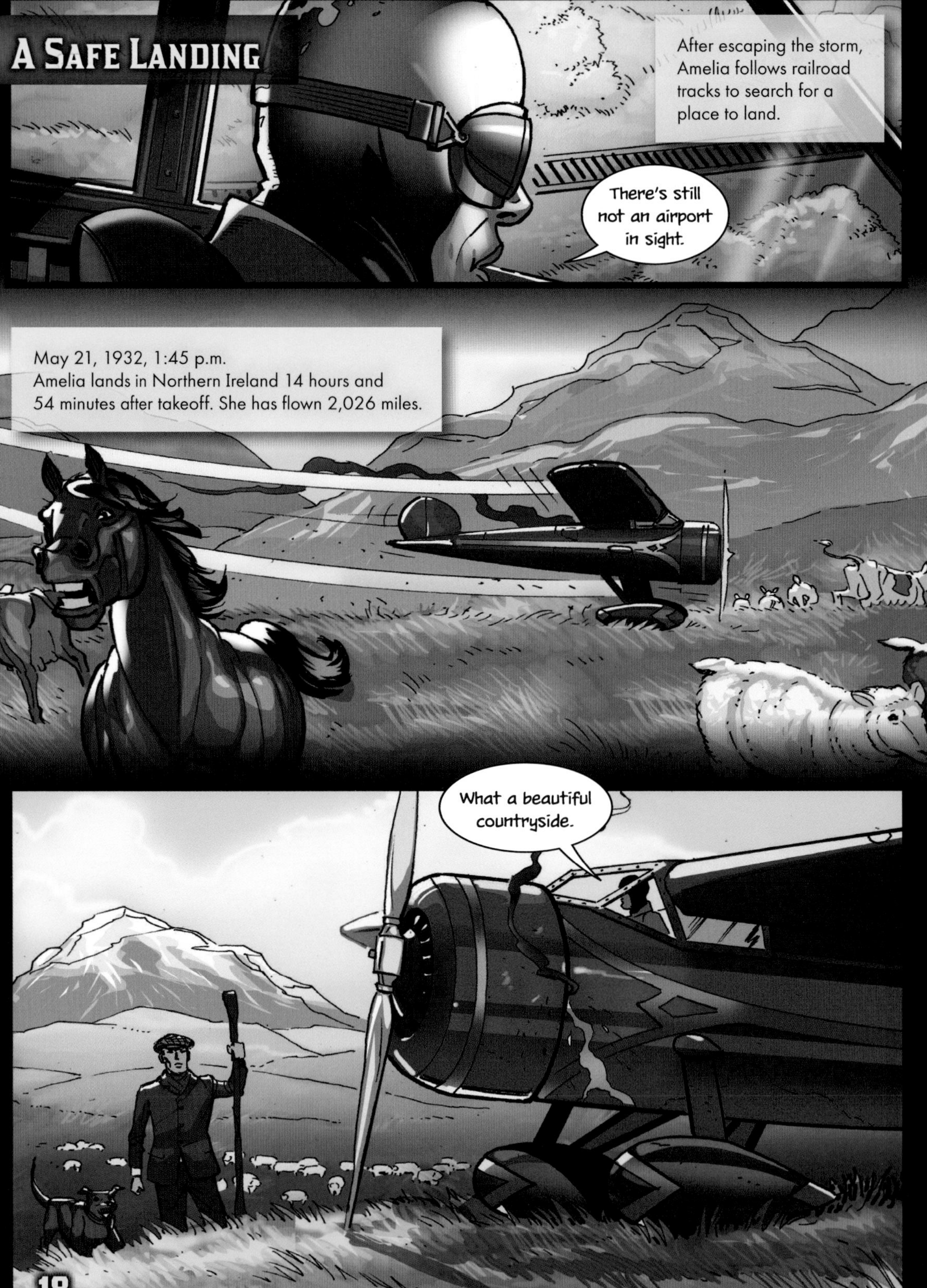
After escaping the storm, Amelia follows railroad tracks to search for a place to land.
There's still not an airport in sight.
May 21, 1932, 1:45 p.m.
Amelia lands in Northern Ireland 14 hours and 54 minutes after takeoff. She has flown 2,026 miles.
What a beautiful countryside.

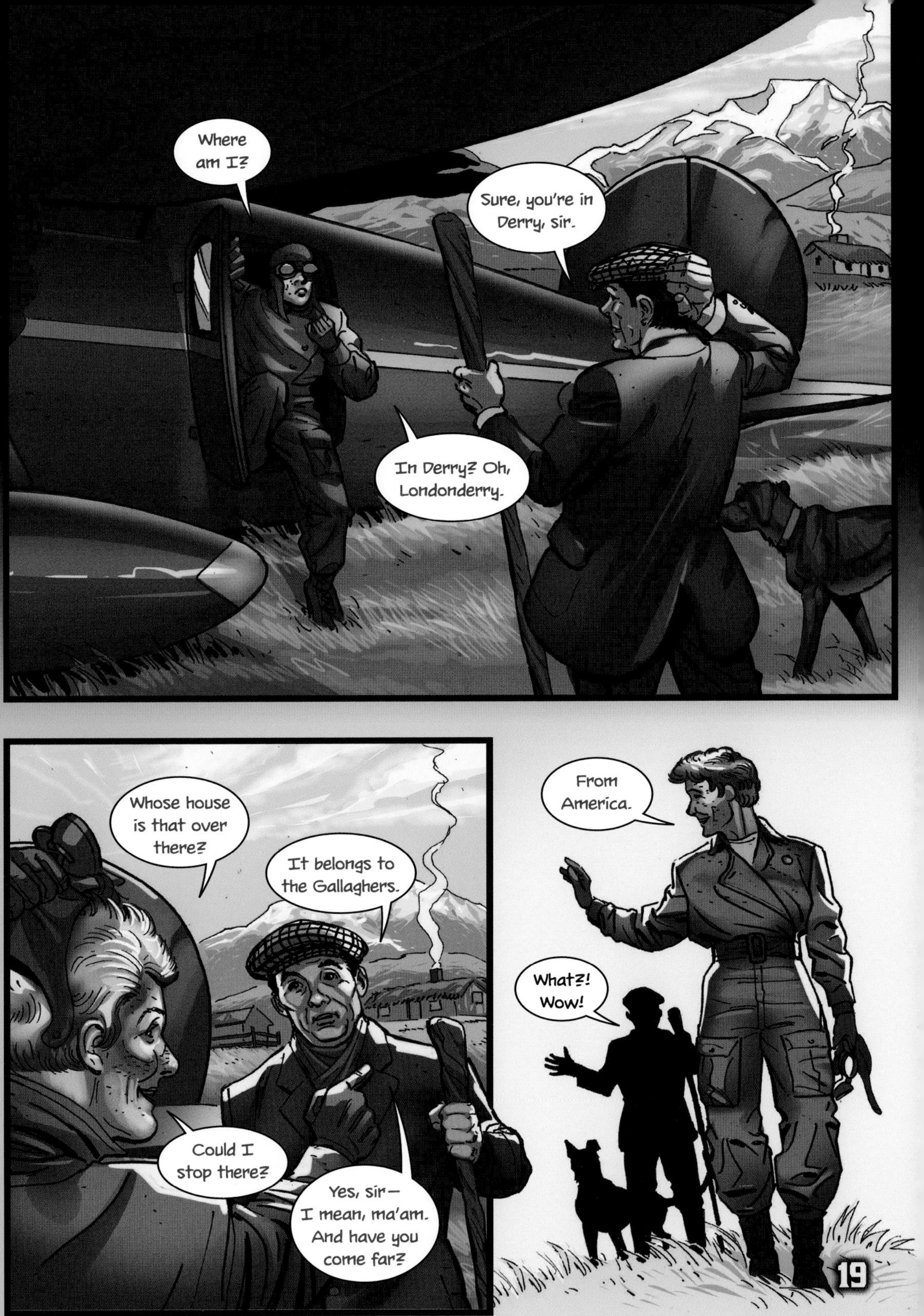

Where am I?
Sure, you're in Derry, sir.
In Derry? Oh, Londonderry.
Whose house is that over there?
It belongs to the Gallaghers.
Could I stop there?
Yes, sir— I mean, ma'am. And have you come far?
From America.
What?! Wow!

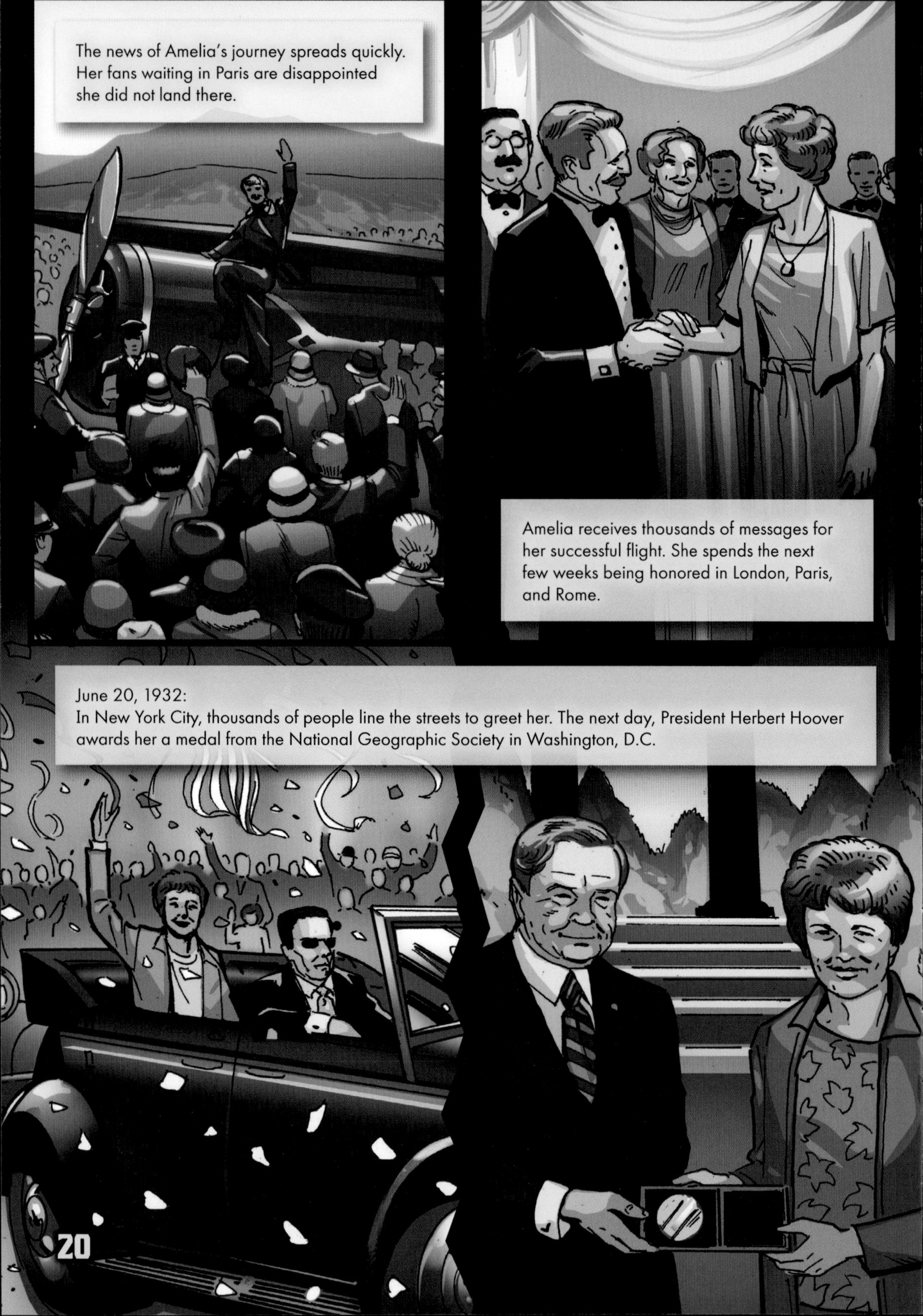
The news of Amelia's journey spreads quickly. Her fans waiting in Paris are disappointed she did not land there.
Amelia receives thousands of messages for her successful flight. She spends the next few weeks being honored in London, Paris, and Rome.
June 20, 1932:
In New York City, thousands of people line the streets to greet her. The next day, President Herbert Hoover awards her a medal from the National Geographic Society in Washington, D.C.

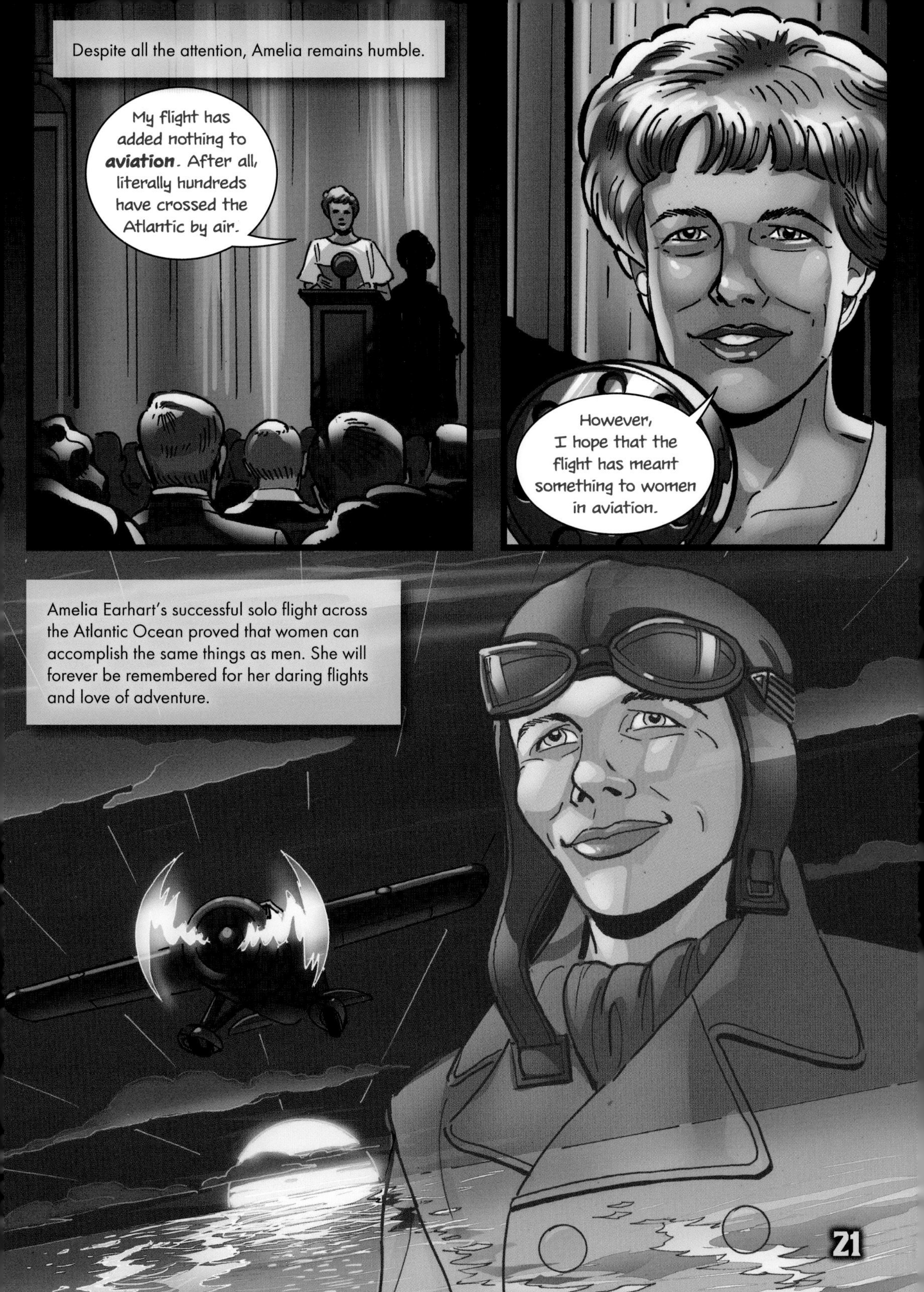
Despite all the attention, Amelia remains humble.
My flight has added nothing to **aviation**. After all, literally hundreds have crossed the Atlantic by air.
However, I hope that the flight has meant something to women in aviation.
Amelia Earhart's successful solo flight across the Atlantic Ocean proved that women can accomplish the same things as men. She will forever be remembered for her daring flights and love of adventure.

More About Amelia Earhart

- Amelia decided not to bring a radio on the Vega. She did not know how to communicate using the codes needed at the time.

- Amelia chose to take off on May 20 because it was the same day that Charles Lindbergh began his flight five year earlier.

- Amelia's successful solo flight made her the first person in the world to fly over the Atlantic Ocean twice. It also broke the record for the fastest flight across the Atlantic.

- Amelia's flight broke the record for the longest distance flown by a female pilot.

- In July 1937, Amelia disappeared while trying to fly around the world. Her plane was never found.

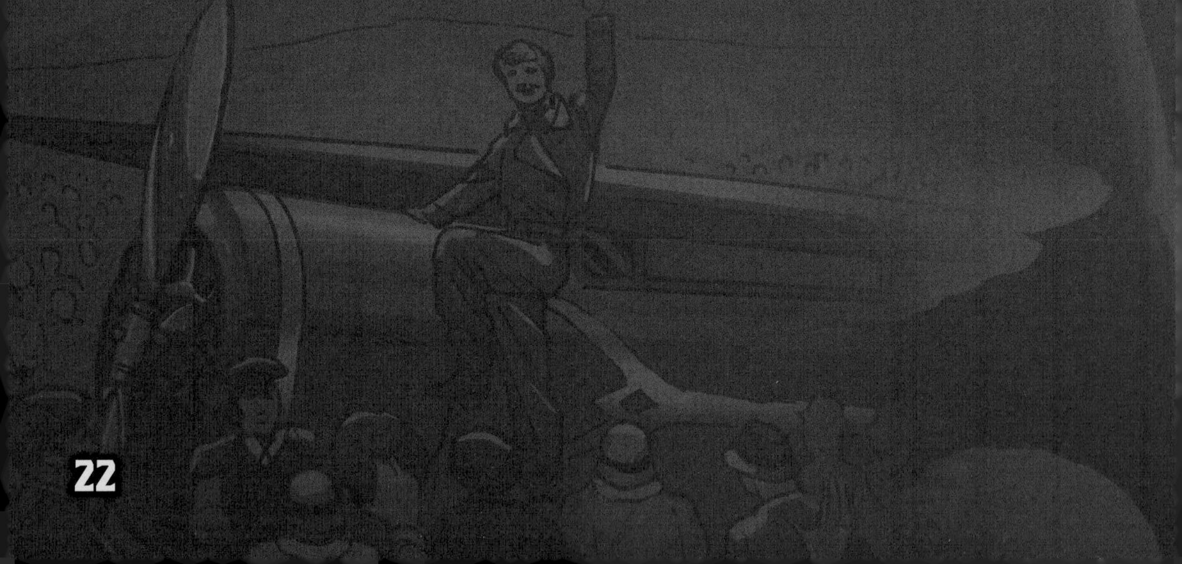

GLOSSARY

altimeter—an instrument that measures how high a plane is from the ground

altitude—the height of something above the ground or sea level

aviation—relating to airplanes and flying

critics—people who disagree with something

exhaust manifold—a part of an airplane that collects the exhaust gases from the engine and sends them to the exhaust pipe

fuel gauge—an instrument that measures the amount of gasoline in a tank

fuselage—the main body of an aircraft where the crew, passengers, and cargo are carried

ignites—catches fire

mechanic—a person who repairs machines, such as vehicles or airplanes

navigation—relating to determining your location

spin—a plane's rapid drop in altitude, in which the aircraft may begin to twirl around as it falls

vibrations—shaking movements

weld—a spot where two pieces of metal are joined together

TO LEARN MORE

AT THE LIBRARY

Anderson, Jameson. *Amelia Earhart: Legendary Aviator*. Mankato, Minn.: Capstone Press, 2007.

Orr, Tamra B. *Amelia Earhart*. New York, N.Y.: Scholastic, 2015.

Taylor, Sarah Stewart. *Amelia Earhart: This Broad Ocean*. New York, N.Y.: Disney/Hyperion, 2010.

ON THE WEB

Learning more about Amelia Earhart is as easy as 1, 2, 3.

1. Go to www.factsurfer.com.
2. Enter "Amelia Earhart" into the search box.
3. Click the "Surf" button and you will see a list of related web sites.

With factsurfer.com, finding more information is just a click away.

INDEX

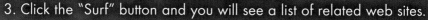

altimeter, 7, 9
Atlantic Ocean, 4, 21
Balchen, Bernt, 5
Europe, 6, 7
exhaust manifold, 7, 11, 12, 13, 15
Gorski, Eddie, 5
Harbour Grace, Newfoundland, 4, 5, 7
historical quotes, 5, 6, 19, 21
Hoover, Herbert (president), 20
Ireland, 5, 16
landing, 5, 6, 7, 18, 20
Le Bourget Airport, 14
Lindbergh, Charles, 4, 5
Lockheed Vega 5B, 4, 5, 7, 9
Londonderry, 19
National Geographic Society, 20
Northern Ireland, 18
Paris, France, 5, 14, 20
Putnam, George, 5